Regulation of Bitcoin in Selected Jurisdictions

Global Legal Research Directorate Staff

I. Introduction

This report surveys forty foreign jurisdictions and the European Union, reporting on any regulations or statements from central banks or government offices on the handling of bitcoins as well as any significant use of bitcoins in business transactions.[1] Topics covered include whether bitcoins are recognized as legal tender, the possibility of negative impacts on the national currency, concerns about fraud, and how transactions using the Bitcoin system are viewed by tax authorities.

Of those countries surveyed, only a very few, notably China and Brazil, have specific regulations applicable to bitcoin use. There is widespread concern about the Bitcoin system's possible impact on national currencies, its potential for criminal misuse, and the implications of its use for taxation. Overall, the findings of this report reveal that the debate over how to deal with this new virtual currency is still in its infancy.

II. Jurisdictional Surveys

Alderney (Channel Islands)

There are no official statements on the Alderney government's website regarding its position towards the bitcoin, and it appears to be unregulated on the island. However, journalists have reportedly obtained documents indicating that Alderney is trying to take the lead and become the central hub for the bitcoin, by minting and issuing physical bitcoins and creating an international center with a bitcoin storage vault service that complies with anti-money laundering rules. As Alderney is a Crown Dependency of the United Kingdom, the UK's Royal Mint would need to be involved in issuing any physical currency, and the Head of New Development at the Royal Mint confirmed to the *Financial Times* that discussions about issuing the currency have occurred, but at this time, it remains merely a concept.[2]

---

[1] Bitcoin is a peer-to-peer payment system and digital cryptocurrency developed in 2009. This report follows the convention established by the official Bitcoin website of capitalizing "Bitcoin" when describing the concept of Bitcoin, or the entire network itself, and not capitalizing "bitcoin" when describing the bitcoin as a unit of account (often abbreviated BTC or XBT). *Some Bitcoin Words You Might Hear*, BITCOIN, http://bitcoin.org/en/ vocabulary (last visited Jan. 15, 2014).

[2] Jane Wild, *Alderney Looks to Cash in on Virtual Bitcoins with Royal Mint Reality*, FINANCIAL TIMES (London) (Nov. 29, 2013), http://www.ft.com/intl/cms/s/0/4903fc9a-591f-11e3-a7cb-00144feab dc0.html#axzz2piwDriV8.

Argentina

Under the National Constitution of Argentina[3] the only authority capable of issuing legal currency is the Central Bank.[4] Bitcoins are not legal currency strictly speaking, since they are not issued by the government monetary authority and are not legal tender. Therefore, they may be considered money but not legal currency, since they are not a mandatory means of cancelling debts or obligations. Although bitcoins are not specifically regulated, they are increasingly being used in Argentina, a country that has strict control over foreign currencies.[5] According to some experts[6] a bitcoin may be considered a good or a thing under the Civil Code,[7] and transactions with bitcoins may be governed by the rules of the sale of goods under the Civil Code.[8]

Australia

In June 2013, a senior Australian Taxation Office (ATO) official told *The Australian Financial Review* that the ATO is monitoring the bitcoin, including "its volatility, how widely it is accepted, its interaction with conventional currencies through exchange mechanisms and international developments."[9] The article indicated that the ATO intends to catch misconduct and subject the currency to the same taxation requirements that apply to conventional commercial transactions, including the Goods and Services Tax (GST). Another ATO spokesman said that those speculating in bitcoins may face tax implications and should "keep detailed records and evidence about what trades they make and the source of any assumptions about the value of any transaction in Australian dollars."[10]

In December 2013, the governor of the Reserve Bank of Australia (RBA) indicated in an interview with *The Australian Financial Review* that the bitcoin has not caused the RBA any

---

[3] CONSTITUCIÓN DE LA NACIÓN ARGENTINA [NATIONAL CONSTITUTION OF ARGENTINA], Aug. 22, 1994, art. 75, para. 6, http://www.constitution.org/cons/argentin.htm.

[4] Ley No. 24.144, Carta Orgánica del Banco Central de la República Argentina [Law No. 24,144, Charter of the Central Bank of the Republic of Argentina] art. 30, Oct. 13, 1992 http://www.infoleg.gob.ar/infolegInternet/anexos/0-4999/542/norma.htm. (Arg.)

[5] *Bitcoin: Fiebre Argentina por la Máquina de Dinero Digital* [*Bitcoin: Argentine Fever for the Digital Money Machine*], LA NACIÓN (June 30, 2013), http://www.lanacion.com.ar/1596773-bitcoin-pasion-argentina-por-la-nueva-maquina-de-hacer-billetes-digitales; *Argentina es uno de los países que más usa el bitcoin* [*Argentina Is One of the Countries That Uses the Bitcoin*], CLARÍN (Dec. 31, 2013), http://www.clarin.com/sociedad/Argentina-paises-Bitcoin-moneda-virtual_0_1057694271.html.

[6] *See, e.g.,* Andres Chomczyk, *Situación Legal del Bitcoin en Argentina*, ELBITCOIN.ORG, (Oct. 10, 2013), http://elbitcoin.org/situacion-legal-de-bitcoin-en-argentina./.

[7] CÓDIGO CIVIL [CIVIL CODE] art. 2311, http://www.infoleg.gov.ar/infolegInternet/anexos/105000-109999/109481/texact.htm (last visited Dec. 31, 2013) (Arg.).

[8] *Id.* art. 1323.

[9] Kate Walsh & Jason Murphy, *ATO Targets Bitcoin Users*, AUSTRALIAN FINANCIAL REVIEW (June 24, 2013), http://www.afr.com/p/technology/ato_targets_bitcoin_users_oawpzLQHDz2vEUWtvYLTWI.

[10] Liz Tay, *The ATO Says Bitcoins Have Been Taxable Since the Get-Go*, BUSINESS INSIDER AUSTRALIA (June 25, 2013), http://www.businessinsider.com.au/the-ato-says-bitcoins-have-been-taxable-since-the-get-go-2013-6.

"material problem yet," but that there were risks for speculators.[11]   He said that there was nothing to stop people holding or transacting in other currencies in Australia, including the bitcoin.

In October 2013, an Australian Bitcoin bank was hacked, resulting in the theft of over US$1 million of the currency.[12]

Belgium

There are no specific laws or regulations regarding Bitcoin in Belgium.

The Belgian Finance Minister, in response to a question by a Belgian senator, stated in July 2013 that while the Bitcoin system seems to be somewhat problematic as a potential tool for money laundering and other illegal activities, such problems should not be overstated.   He also stated that, based on studies from the Belgian central bank (Banque nationale de Belgique) and the European Central Bank, the bitcoin does not present any significant risks to price stability, to the financial system in general, or to its individual users.   Finally, in this same statement, the Minister of Finance indicated that government intervention with regard to the Bitcoin system does not appear necessary at the present time.[13]

Brazil

On October 9, 2013, Brazil enacted Law No. 12,865, which created the possibility for the normalization of mobile payment systems and the creation of electronic currencies, including the bitcoin.   The Law provides, among other things, for the payment arrangements and payment institutions that comprise the Brazilian Payment System (Sistema de Pagamentos Brasileiro, SPB).[14]

Law No. 12,865 defines "payment arrangement" as a set of rules and procedures that regulate the rendering of a particular service to the public that is accepted by more than one recipient, through direct access by end users, payers, and recipients.[15]   "Payment institution" is defined as a legal entity that, by adhering to one or more payment arrangements, has as a principal or

---

[11] Bianca Hartge-Hazelman, *Glenn Stevens Says Bitcoins Show Promise, But So Did Tulips*, THE AUSTRALIAN FINANCIAL REVIEW (Dec. 13, 2013), http://www.afr.com/p/national/glenn_stevens_says_bitcoins_show_GWLQFcefJfF4Rmi E0Z08AJ; *Full Transcript: Glenn Stevens on the $A, Rates and Growth*, THE AUSTRALIAN FINANCIAL REVIEW (Dec. 13, 2013), http://www.afr.com/p/national/economy/full_transcript_glenn_stevens_on_g8FIuePVTxTVnSVJnv5knM.

[12] Jim Urquhart, *Bit-Heist: Over $1mn in Bitcoins Stolen from Australian Online Bank*, RT.COM (Nov. 8, 2013), http://rt.com/news/bitcoin-hacking-stolen-million-417/.

[13] Question écrite no. 5-8723 de Martine Taelman du 16 avril 2013 au ministre des Finances [Written Question No. 5-8723 of April 16, 2013, from Martine Taelman to the Minister of Finance], SÉNAT DE BELGIQUE (July 31, 2013), http://www.senate.be/www/?MIval=/index_senate&MENUID=23100&LANG=fr (search by question no.).

[14] Lei No. 12.865, de 9 de Outubro de 2013 [Law No. 12,865 of October 9, 2013], http://www.receita.fazenda.gov. br/Legislacao/leis/2013/lei12865.htm (Braz.).

[15] *Id.* art. 6(I).

secondary activity, alternatively or cumulatively, one of the activities listed in article 6(III). "Electronic currency" is defined as resources stored on a device or electronic system that allow the end user to perform a payment transaction.[16]

Article 7 lists the principles that must be observed by the payment arrangements and payment institutions, according to the parameters to be established by the Brazilian Central Bank in accordance with the directives of the National Monetary Council (Conselho Monetário Nacional, CMN). Article 9 defines the competence of the Brazilian Central Bank, pursuant to the directives established by the CMN. Article 11 determines that the penalties provided for in the legislation applicable to financial institutions applies to the infractions set forth in Law No. 12,865 and in the directives and norms established, respectively, by the CMN and the Brazilian Central Bank.

Law No. 12,865 authorizes the Brazilian Central Bank to issue the necessary norms and instructions for the fulfillment of its provisions; this must be done within 180 days of the publication of the Law and in accordance with the guidelines established by the CMN.[17]

Canada

Canada does not have a specific law or regulation that regulates bitcoins. In an emailed statement to *The Wall Street Journal* in January 2014, a Canadian official from Canada's Department of Finance stated that Canada does not consider bitcoins to be legal tender. The official reportedly stated that "[o]nly Canadian bank notes and coins are recognized as legal tender in Canada. Bitcoin digital 'currency' is not legal tender in Canada."[18] However, the official also stated that the government of Canada would continue to "monitor developments involving virtual currencies."[19]

The Wall Street Journal article also quoted a spokesman for Bank of Canada, Canada's central bank, who stated that Bank of Canada has been taking a greater interest in bitcoins and other alternative forms of payment owing to "financial stability considerations."[20] According to the spokesman,

---

[16] *Id.* art. 6(VI).

[17] *Id.* art. 15.

[18] David George-Cosh, *Canada Says Bitcoin Isn't Legal Tender*, THE WALL STREET JOURNAL (Jan. 16, 2014), http://blogs.wsj.com/canadarealtime/2014/01/16/canada-says-bitcoin-isnt-legal-tender/.

[19] Id.

[20] Id.

[s]maller, stand-alone payment systems for which there are many substitutes – like bitcoin – should generally require much less intensive oversight and regulation because they pose much less risk to the Canadian financial system as a whole. . . . Nevertheless, these payment systems should be designed and operated to meet the needs of Canadians which would include convenience and ease of use, price, reliability, safety, and effective redress mechanisms.[21]

In April 2013, Canada's Revenue Agency reportedly stated that users of bitcoins will have to pay tax on transactions in the digital currency, based on two separate tax rules that apply to barter transactions and things that are bought and sold for speculative purposes.[22] According to another news report, the Financial Transactions and Reports Analysis Centre of Canada (FINTRAC), Canada's financial intelligence unit, sent out letters to a number of major Canadian Bitcoin service operators stating that their bitcoin exchanges were not at this time "engaged as a money services business in Canada as per the Proceeds of Crime (Money Laundering) and Terrorist Financing and its associated Regulations," and would not be subject to its rules or have to be registered with FINTRAC.[23]

Chile

According to news reports, there are no merchants that accept bitcoins in Chile as of yet. Buying virtual currencies in Chile is still very cumbersome.[24] However, there is a community of information technology professionals who are promoting the use of bitcoins, and have even opened the first virtual money exchange store in the country. Interest in acquiring bitcoins is slowly growing. However, because there is no regulation on the use of bitcoins, transactions are informal in nature and mainly conducted among friends.[25]

In 2013, a group of American Libertarians founded a self-sustaining organic farming community called Galt's Gulch Chile in central Chile with an economy based on bitcoins.[26]

---

[21] Id.

[22] *Revenue Canada Says BitCoins Aren't Tax Exempt*, CBC NEWS (Apr. 26, 2013), http://www.cbc.ca/news/business/revenue-canada-says-bitcoins-aren-t-tax-exempt-1.1395075.

[23] Jasper Hamill, *Canadian Regulators Welcome US Bitcoin Refugees with Open Arms,* REGISTER (May 20, 2013), http://www.theregister.co.uk/2013/05/20/canada_welcomes_bitcoin_traders_fintrac_letter/.

[24] *Bitcoin, la Revolución del Dinero* [*Bitcoin, the Money Revolution*], CAPITAL ONLINE (Aug. 12, 2013), http://www.capital.cl/negocios/bitcoin-la-revolucion-del-dinero/.

[25] *Moneda Virtual Bitcoin Crece en el Mundo y Suma Adeptos en Chile* [*Virtual Money Bitcoin Grows in the World and Adds Followers*], EL MERCURIO (Nov. 18, 2013), http://diario.elmercurio.com/detalle/index.asp?id={b967addd-8fbc-495b-be4e-eb4e60603fde (registration required).

[26] *Bitcoin Paradise*, THE ECONOMIST (Dec. 25, 2013), http://www.economist.com/blogs/schumpeter/2013/12/libertarian-enclaves (registration required); *Galt's Gulch Chile Becomes First Libertarian Community Accepting Bitcoin*, GALT'S GULCH CHILE (Nov. 12, 2013), http://galtsgulchchile.com/News/Detail/10.

China

On December 3, 2013, the central bank of China and four other central government ministries and commissions jointly issued the Notice on Precautions Against the Risks of Bitcoins.[27] Defining it as a special "virtual commodity," the Notice said that by nature the bitcoin is not a currency and should not be circulated and used in the market as a currency.[28]

Banks and payment institutions in China are prohibited from dealing in bitcoins. The Notice required that, at this stage, financial and payment institutions may not use bitcoin pricing for products or services, buy or sell bitcoins, or provide direct or indirect bitcoin-related services to customers, including registering, trading, settling, clearing, or other services; accepting bitcoins or using bitcoins as a clearing tool; and trading bitcoins with Chinese yuan or foreign currencies.[29]

The Notice further required strengthening the oversight of Internet websites providing bitcoin registration, trading, and other services. It also warned about the risks of using the Bitcoin system for money laundering.[30]

Croatia

On December 6, 2013, the Croatian National Bank (CNB) reportedly conducted a discussion on the circulation of digital currencies and concluded that the bitcoin is not illegal in Croatia:[31]

> [CNB] said that it is not electronic money since it's not debt to the issuer (although it has some similarities with electronic money), and that it is not legal tender in Croatia but can be legally used. Croatian kunas (HRK) are the official means of payment in Croatia, but in some cases payment in other currencies is allowed, such as when person/company from Croatia is transacting with another entity from outside of Croatia.[32]

No specific guidelines were issued and no formal statement was found on CNB's website. According to the same report,

---

[27] 关于防范比特币风险的通知 [Notice on Precautions Against the Risks of Bitcoins] (issued by the People's Bank of China, the Ministry of Industry and Information Technology, China Banking Regulatory Commission, China Securities Regulatory Commission, and China Insurance Regulatory Commission, Dec. 3, 2013) YIN FA, 2013, No. 289, http://www.pbc.gov.cn/publish/goutongjiaoliu/524/2013/20131205153156832222251/20131205153156832222 251_.html (China). An unofficial English summary of the Notice is available at BTC CHINA, https://vip.btcchina. com/page/bocnotice2013 (last visited Jan. 13, 2014).

[28] *Id.* § 1.

[29] *Id.* § 2.

[30] *Id.* § 3–4.

[31] *Croatia Allowed to Use Bitcoin*, COINSPOT.RU (Dec. 16, 2013), http://coinspot.ru/news/xorvatiya-razreshila-ispolzovanie-bitkoina/ (in Russian).

[32] *Croatian Central Bank Establishes that Bitcoin Is Legal in Croatia*, REDDIT.COM (Dec. 9, 2013), http://www. reddit.com/r/Bitcoin/comments/1sjgby/croatian_central_bank_establishes_that_bitcoin_is/.

CNB commented that money is [a] social institution, and that it's not unusual that money is evolving as influenced by the Internet, and established that Bitcoin is at the moment not regulated or directly monitored, but that regulation will probably in the future fall under the jurisdiction of central banks."[33]

Cyprus

The use of bitcoins is not regulated in Cyprus. On December 11, 2013, the Central Bank of Cyprus issued a statement on bitcoins, stating that "it considers the use of any kind of virtual money as particularly dangerous, given that it is not under any regulatory system and its operation is unchecked."[34]

Denmark

Denmark's Finanstilsynet (Financial Supervisory Authority) has issued a statement rejecting the bitcoin as a currency and stating that it will not regulate bitcoin use.[35] In its statement the Finanstilsynet emphasizes that it has evaluated the use of the Bitcoin system and found that Bitcoin does not fall under any of the financial services categories, including the issuing of electronic money, payment for services, currency exchanges, or the issuing of mortages; thus, Bitcoin activity is not covered under current financial regulation.[36] This statement by the Financial Supervisory Authority suggests that Bitcoin should be treated as an electronic service and earnings from its use would therefore be taxable. However, the Danish Tax Authority has not published any comment as to whether Bitcoin earnings should be taxed.

Estonia

In Estonia, the use of bitcoins is not regulated or otherwise controlled by the government. Because of the Bitcoin service's growing popularity and increasing use by the country's population, however, the Bank of Estonia (the nation's central bank) monitors financial arrangements that use Bitcoin.[37] According to Google's search statistics, Estonia is the country with the second largest number of Internet searches for the term "Bitcoin"; Russia has the most such searches.[38]

---

[33] *Id.*

[34] *Cyprus Central Bank Warns About Risks in Use of Bitcoin*, FAMAGUSTA GAZETTE (Dec. 10, 2012), http://fama gusta-gazette.com/cyprus-central-bank-warns-about-risks-in-use-of-bitcoin-p21692-69.htm.

[35] *Advarsel mod virtuelle valutaer (bitcoin m.fl.)* [*Warnings Against Digital Currencies (Bitcoins etc.)*], FINANSTILSYNET (Dec. 17, 2013), http://www.finanstilsynet.dk/da/Nyhedscenter/Pressemeddelelser/2013/Advarsel-mod-virtuelle-valutaer-bitcom-mfl-2013.aspx.

[36] *Id.*

[37] *What the Bank of Estonia Thinks About Bitcoin*, DV.EE (Dec. 19, 2013), http://www.dv.ee/article/2013/12/19/chto-bank-jestonii-dumaet-o-bitkoine (in Russian).

[38] Emma Rowley, *Russians Most Interested in Bitcoin, Searches Show*, THE TELEGRAPH (Apr. 6, 2013), http://www. telegraph.co.uk/finance/economics/9976524/Russians-most-interested-in-Bitcoin-searches-show.html.

On December 19, 2013, the Estonian business information Web portal Dv.ee published comments by Michkel Nymmel, the head of the Payment Processing Department of the Bank of Estonia, concerning the increased use of various financial schemes related to digital currencies. Nymmel said that according to Bank of Estonia estimates, the bitcoin does not create any threat to financial or price stability because of its limited virtual area of circulation. He did warn that "[w]hile Bitcoin provides users with an alternative to traditional payment systems, the bank believes that there are numerous risks to customers owing to [the] absence of security mechanisms and credit protection measures."[39]

European Union

The European Union (EU) has passed no specific legislation relative to the status of the bitcoin as a currency. In October 2012, the European Central Bank issued a report on virtual currency schemes that discusses the Bitcoin system and briefly analyzes its legal status under existing EU legislation.[40] Some commentators have suggested that the bitcoin may fall within the definition of the Electronic Money Directive 2009/110/EC.[41] That Directive defines electronic money based on three criteria: (a) electronic storage, (b) issuance upon receipt of funds, and (c) acceptance as a means of payment by a legal or natural person other than the issuer.[42] The report states that the bitcoin meets the first and third criteria but not the second. Other experts suggest that the bitcoin falls within the definition of Payment Services Directive 2007/64/EC.[43] In general, this Directive prescribes rules related to the execution of payments through electronic money. However, as the report concludes, the bitcoin falls outside the scope of Directive 2007/64/EC because this Directive does not deal with electronic money and because payment institutions introduced by the Directive are not permitted to issue electronic money.[44]

The report also notes that the bitcoin issue has been raised with the European Commission's Payments Committee.[45]

On December 13, 2013, the European Banking Authority (EBA), the regulatory agency of the EU responsible for advising EU institutions on banking, e-money regulation, and payments, issued a warning on the dangers associated with transactions, such as buying, holding, or trading

---

[39] DV.EE, *supra* note 37.

[40] EUROPEAN CENTRAL BANK, VIRTUAL CURRENCY SCHEMES (Oct. 2012), http://www.ecb.europa.eu/pub/pdf/other/virtualcurrencyschemes201210en.pdf.

[41] Directive 2009/110/EC of the European Parliament and of the Council of 16 September 2009 on the Taking Up, Pursuit and Prudential Supervision of the Business of Electronic Money Institutions, Amending Directives 2005/60/EC and 2006/48/EC and Repealing Directive 2000/46/EC, 2009 O.J. (L 267) 7, http://eur-lex.europa.eu/LexUriServ/LexUriServ.do?uri=OJ:L:2009:267:0007:0017:EN:PDF.

[42] *Id.* art. 2(2).

[43] Directive 2007/64/EC of the European Parliament and of the Council of 13 November 2007 on Payment Services in the Internal Market, Amending Directives 97/7/EC, 2002/65/EC, 2005/60/EC and 2006/48/EC and Repealing Directive 97/5/EC, 2007 O.J. (L 319) 1, http://eur-lex.europa.eu/LexUriServ/LexUriServ.do?uri=OJ:L:2007:319:0001:0036:EN:PDF.

[44] EUROPEAN CENTRAL BANK, *supra* note 40, at 43.

[45] *Id.*

virtual currencies. The EBA pointed out that since the bitcoin is not regulated, consumers are not protected and are at risk of losing their money and that consumers may still be liable for taxes when using virtual currencies.[46]

Finland

The Finish Tax Authority, Vero Skatt, has issued instructions for the taxation of virtual currencies, including the bitcoin. When transferred to another currency, the rules on taxation of capital gains apply. When the currency is used as a form of payment for goods and services, it is treated as a trade, and the increase in value that the currency might have gained after it was obtained is taxable.[47] The sale of bitcoins at a loss in value compared to the original purchase price is not deductible under the Finish Income Taxation Act, because such a loss in value is not specifically described as deductible in the Act.[48]

France

There are no specific laws or regulations regarding the Bitcoin system in France.

Banque de France, France's central bank, has recently released a report on the bitcoin, warning about the dangers of such "virtual currencies."[49] This report explains that the bitcoin cannot be considered a real currency or means of payment under current French laws,[50] and criticizes it as a vehicle for speculation as well as an instrument for money laundering and other illegal activities.[51] This report also suggests that the conversion between the bitcoin and real currencies should be considered a payment service, which therefore could only be performed by payment service providers authorized and supervised by the French Prudential Supervisory Authority (Autorité de contrôle prudentiel et de resolution).[52] This would help limit the risk of fraud during the sale or purchase of bitcoins, and also help ensure that such operations are subject to existing regulations regarding money laundering and terrorism financing.[53]

---

[46] Press Release, European Banking Authority, EBA Warns Consumers on Virtual Currencies (Dec. 13, 2013), http://www.eba.europa.eu/-/eba-warns-consumers-on-virtual-currencies.

[47] Vero Skatt, *Inkomstbeskattning av virtuella valutor* [*Income Taxation of Virtual Currencies*] (Aug. 28, 2013, http://www.vero.fi/sv-FI/Detaljerade_skatteanvisningar/Inkomstbeskattning_av_personkunder/Inkomst beskattning_av_virtuella_valutor%2828454%29.

[48] *Id.*

[49] Banque de France, Les dangers liés au développement des monnaies virtuelles: l'exemple du bitcoin [The Dangers of the Development of Virtual Currencies: The Bitcoin Example], FOCUS No. 10 (Dec. 5, 2013), http://www.banque-france.fr/fileadmin/user_upload/banque_de_france/publications/Focus-10-stabilite-financiere.pdf.

[50] *Id.* at 1.

[51] *Id.* at 2–3.

[52] *Id.* at 6.

[53] *Id.*

A 2011 court decision that is mentioned in the Banque de France report found that a company that acted as an exchange for bitcoins should be considered a payment service provider, subject to oversight from the French Prudential Supervisory Authority.[54]

Germany

The German Federal Financial Supervisory Authority (Bundesamt für Finanzdienstleistungen, BaFin) issued a communication on bitcoins on December 19, 2013.[55] According to BaFin, bitcoins are legally binding financial instruments that fall into the category of units of account, according to the first sentence of section 1(11) of the German Banking Act.[56] Within that group of financial instruments, the bitcoin is related to foreign currencies. Accordingly, bitcoins are units that are not expressed in the form of legal tender. Instead, they are units of value that have the function of private means of payment within private trading exchanges, or they are substitute currencies that are used as a means of payment in multilateral trading transactions on the basis of legal agreements of private law. The manner in which bitcoins are currently given as payment, accepted as payment, or "mined"[57] does not require bank supervisory licensing. However, licensing could become necessary under various circumstances, such as the creation or maintenance of a market in bitcoins.

The tax treatment of bitcoins has been discussed in some statements by the Federal Ministry of Finance. Among the opinions voiced by the Ministry is a statement on the possibility of value-added tax liability for bitcoin transfers, the lack of income tax effects for the underlying transaction when bitcoins are used as a means of payment, and the lack of long-term capital gains liability for bitcoins that are held for longer than one year.[58]

Greece

No specific legislation on bitcoins exists in Greece, nor has the National Bank of Greece issued any statement on bitcoins. A private company has listed a few businesses that accept bitcoins as a form of payment, however.[59]

---

[54] *Id.*, *referring to* SAS Macaraja c/ SA Crédit Industriel et Commercial, Tribunal de commerce [Commercial Tribunal] Créteil, 2è ch., Dec. 6, 2011.

[55] Jens Münzer, *Bitcoins: Aufsichtliche Bewertung und Risiken für Nutzer* [*Bitcoins: Supervisory Evaluation and Risks for Users*], BAFIN (Dec. 19, 2013), http://www.bafin.de/SharedDocs/Veroeffentlichungen/DE/Fachartikel/2014/fa_bj_1401_bitcoins.html.

[56] Kreditwesengesetz [Banking Act] (updated Sept. 9, 1998), BUNDESGESETZBLATT I at 2776, as amended, http://www.gesetze-im-internet.de/kredwg/index.html (Ger.).

[57] "Bitcoin mining is the process of making computer hardware do mathematical calculations for the Bitcoin network to confirm transactions and increase security. As a reward for their services, Bitcoin miners can collect transaction fees for the transactions they confirm, along with newly created bitcoins." BITCOIN, *supra* note 1.

[58] Franz Nestler, *Deutschland erkennt Bitcoins als privates Geld an* [*Germany Recognizes Bitcoins as Private Money*], FRANKFURTER ALLGEMEINE ZEITUNG (Aug. 16, 2013), http://www.faz.net/aktuell/finanzen/devisen-rohstoffe/digitale-waehrung-deutschland-erkennt-bitcoins-als-privates-geld-an-12535059.html.

[59] *Bitcoin Greek Register*, BITCOINX.GR, http://bitcoinx.gr/apps/katalogos/ (in Greek) (last visited Jan. 16, 2014).

Hong Kong

As of January 8, 2014, Hong Kong had not adopted any legislation specifically regulating the Bitcoin system, while "the Government and the relevant regulators have been keeping a close watch on the use of bitcoins locally."[60] The Secretary for Financial Services and the Treasury addressed this issue in the Legislative Council on January 8 with the statement that, "[l]ike many other regions, Hong Kong at present has no legislation directly regulating bitcoins and other virtual currencies of [a] similar kind. However, our existing laws (such as the Organised and Serious Crimes Ordinance) provide sanctions against unlawful acts involving bitcoins, such as fraud or money laundering."[61]

Iceland

In a written response to Iceland's *Morgunblaðið* newspaper, the Central Bank of Iceland reportedly stated that engaging in foreign exchange trading with bitcoins is prohibited, based on the country's Foreign Exchange Act, which sets forth general restrictions on foreign exchange trading and capital movements between Iceland and other countries. According to the Bank's statement, "[i]t does not appear that the provisions of the Act that exempt goods and services from the aforementioned restrictions can be applied to trading in the bitcoin or that other exemptions from restrictions of the Act apply to such transactions."[62]

India

There appears to be no explicit legal framework that regulates, restricts, or bans bitcoins in India. However, India's central bank recently cautioned the public about the possible risks of cybersecurity attacks and money laundering related to the use of this virtual currency. On December 24, 2013, the Reserve Bank of India (RBI) issued a public notice to "users, holders and traders of virtual currencies (VCs), including Bitcoins," regarding the potential "financial, operational, legal, customer protection and security related risks that they are exposing themselves to."[63] Following the RBI's public advisory, India's largest Bitcoin trading platform,

---

[60] Press Release, Government of Hong Kong, LCQ1: Monitoring the Use of Bitcoins (Jan. 8, 2014), http://www. info.gov.hk/gia/general/201401/08/P201401080357.htm.

[61] *Id.*

[62] *Höftin stöðva viðskipti með Bitcoin* [*Controls Stop Trading in Bitcoin*], MORGUNBLAÐIÐ (Dec. 19, 2013), http://www.mbl.is/vidskipti/frettir/2013/12/19/hoftin_stodva_vidskipti_med_bitcoin/; for a rough translation of this article and comments, *see* Saevarg, *Bitcoin Trading Illegal in Iceland According to Icelandic Central Bank*, REDDIT, http://www.reddit.com/r/Bitcoin/comments/1t8zf3/bitcoin_trading_illegal_in_iceland_according_to/ (last visited Jan. 10, 2014). In connection with Bitcoin mining in Iceland, in particular a business called Cloud Hashing set up in February 2013 that uses over one hundred computers and has mining contracts for 4,500 customers, "keeping 20 percent of its capacity open for its own mining," *see* Russell Brandom, *Inside a $4 Million Icelandic Bitcoin-Mining Consortium*, THE VERGE (Dec. 23, 2013), http://www.theverge.com/2013/12/23/5238128/inside-a-4-million-icelandic-bitcoin-mining-consortium.

[63] Press Release, Reserve Bank of India, RBI Cautions Users of Virtual Currencies Against Risks (Dec. 24, 2013), http://rbi.org.in/scripts/BS_PressReleaseDisplay.aspx?prid=30247; *see also RBI Advisory Puts Brakes On Bitcoin Train In India,* TIMES OF INDIA (Jan. 17, 2014), http://timesofindia.indiatimes.com/business/india-business/RBI-advisory-puts-brakes-on-bitcoin-train-in-India/articleshow/28934501.cms.

BuySellBitCo.in, suspended its operations, citing the RBI's notice.[64] Also, two days after the advisory, India's Enforcement Directorate raided the premises of the person in Ahmedabad who had hosted the Bitcoin trading platform, BuySellBitCo.in.[65] According to news reports, the raid occurred because of alleged violations of India's Foreign Exchange Management Act rules.[66] Recent news reports cite the resumption of operations of some Bitcoin operators and the emergence of new players in the market.[67]

Indonesia

A spokesman for Bank Indonesia reportedly issued a statement on Bitcoin in December 2013, saying that "[b]itcoin is a potential payment method, but it's different than ordinary currency. . . . It is not regulated by the central bank so there are risks. . . . At the moment, we're studying bitcoin and we have no plan to issue a regulation on it."[68]

Ireland

The Central Bank of Ireland has not published a statement on its website regarding bitcoins. However, it was quoted in the Dáil Éireann (the Assembly of Ireland, the principal chamber of the Oireachtas, the Irish Parliament) as stating that it does not regulate bitcoins, and they are not considered to be legal tender within the European Union.

The Revenue Commissioners in Ireland are monitoring the development of the bitcoin and considering its implications for possible taxation, with the most likely areas of taxation being in the taxation of any gains, as well as value-added tax, which is a charge on goods and services. The government did raise concerns about the use of bitcoins and noncompliance with tax laws, but reported that it was advised that "currently, the threat posed to the Exchequer is likely to be small. It is probable too that for some evaders, it represents a new opportunity for existing non-compliance, rather than a new form of evasion."[69]

---

[64] *Bitcoin Exchanges Shut Shop in India*, HINDU (Dec. 26, 2013), http://www.thehindu.com/business/Industry/bitcoin-exchanges-shut-shop-in-india/article5504407.ece.

[65] *First Time in the Country, ED Raids a Bitcoin Seller in Ahmedabad,* DNA INDIA (Dec. 27, 2013), http://www.dnaindia.com/india/report-first-time-in-the-country-ed-raids-a-bitcoin-seller-in-ahmedabad-1941187.

[66] *Id.*

[67] *Indian Bitcoin Operators Resume Operations Cautiously*, HINDU (Jan. 15, 2014), http://www.thehindu.com/business/indian-bitcoin-operators-resume-operations-cautiously/article5578640.ece.

[68] Faisal Maliki Baskoro, *Bitcoin Finds Itty-Bitty Market in Indonesia*, JAKARTA GLOBE (Dec. 1, 2013), http://www.thejakartaglobe.com/business/bitcoin-finds-itty-bitty-market-in-indonesia/.

[69] DÁIL DEBATES 126 (Dec. 10, 2013), http://oireachtasdebates.oireachtas.ie/debates%20authoring/debateswebpack.nsf/takes/dail2013121000054?opendocument (Ir.).

Israel

As of December 23, 2013, Israel had not adopted any specific legislation regulating bitcoins. The Israel Tax Authority, however, has reportedly been considering taxing profits derived from trading in bitcoins. In its opinion, "whoever profits from Bitcoin trading owes tax although at this stage it is not yet clear what model for taxing profits will be used."[70]

According to media reports, officials from the Ministry of Justice and Bank of Israel have been conducting discussions on the implications of using bitcoins, particularly in illicit transactions.[71] While Israeli pro-Bitcoin activists highlight the advantages of using virtual currency,[72] commentators argue that because of current price fluctuations, bitcoins are "not yet a reliable store of value, an important feature of functional currency. . . . [In addition, their] near anonymity makes [them] attractive for illicit transactions as well, a problem that government oversight may be able to address."[73]

An incident of an alleged attempted extortion involving a request for payment in bitcoins was reported on December 19, 2013. At least three Israeli banks have received emails from an unknown individual threatening to release the personal details of millions of their customers unless the payment was made. According to news reports, the Bank of Israel has been cooperating with the Shin Bet security service and the Prime Minister's Office to help secure the banks' computer systems.[74]

Italy

Italy's stance on the Bitcoin system parallels the stance taken by the EU. On October 29, 2002, the European Central Bank published a report titled *Virtual Currency Schemes*,[75] which studies relevant economic and legal aspects of the Bitcoin system. A European Directive of 2009 regulates the use of electronic currencies (including the bitcoin) with the aim of harmonizing payment methods, increasing competition, and facilitating market access.[76] Italy implemented this Directive through Legislative Decree No. 45 of April 16, 2012,[77] which defines the concept

---

[70] Ela Levy-Weinrib, *Government Considers Taxing Bitcoin Profits*, GLOBES (Sept. 12, 2013), http://www. globes.co.il/serveen/globes/docview.asp?did=1000879015.

[71] Niv Elis, *Bank of Israel Mulls Regulating, Recognizing Bitcoin Virtual Currency,* THE JERUSALEM POST (Dec. 3, 2013), http://www.jpost.com/Business/Business-News/Bank-of-Israel-mulls-regulating-recognizing-Bitcoin-virtual-currency-333894; *see also* Irit Avissar, *Banks Ask Regulator for Bitcoin Guidelines*, GLOBES (Dec. 3, 2013), http://www.globes.co.il/serveen/globes/docview.asp?did=1000898665.

[72] *See Introduction to Bitcoin*, ISRAELI BITCOIN ASSOCIATION, http://www.bitcoin.org.il/%d7%9e%d7%91% d7% 95%d7%90-%d7%9c%d7%91%d7%99%d7%98%d7%a7%d7%95%d7%99%d7%9f/ (in Hebrew) (last visited Dec. 23, 2013).

[73] *E.g.*, Elis, *supra* note 71.

[74] Sivan Aizescu, *Israeli Banks Report Extortion Attempt by Hacker Demanding Payoff in Bitcoin*, HAARETZ (Dec. 19, 2013), http://www.haaretz.com/business/.premium-1.564459.

[75] European Central Bank, *supra* note 40.

[76] Directive 2009/110/EC, *supra* note 41.

[77] Decreto Legislativo 16 Aprile 2012, n. 45 [Legislative Decree No. 45 of April 16, 2012], NORMATIVVA, http://www.normattiva.it/uri-res/N2Ls?urr:nir:statodecreto:legislativo:2012;045 (It.).

of electronic currency, including the cases in which it is issued electronically in exchange for funds to be used as a means of payment, and identifies the persons authorized to issue electronic money. The Decree allows the use of electronic currencies in accordance with the EU Directive at the level of the European Central Bank, and by the central banks of European Members, the Italian public administration at the regional and local government levels, and the Italian postal system. However, the use of electronic currency is restricted to banks and electronic money institutions—that is, private legal entities duly authorized and registered by the Central Bank of Italy. Aside from these developments, Italy does not regulate bitcoin use by private individuals, and currently the implementation of initiatives concerning the use of electronic currencies lies with the EU.[78]

Japan

There are at present no laws in Japan regulating the use of bitcoins. Haruhiko Kuroda, governor of the Bank of Japan (BOJ), recently stated that BOJ was "researching issues of bitcoins, but I have nothing to say regarding bitcoins at the moment."[79]

Malaysia

Bank Negara Malaysia officials apparently met with local bitcoin proponents in November 2013 to learn more about the currency.[80] However, no official statement regarding the meeting or the Bank's views of the Bitcoin system was located.

Malta

Malta currently does not have any regulations specifically pertaining to bitcoins, nor does there appear to be any official government statement on the recognition or policy towards the bitcoin. According to news reports, the bitcoin is not deemed as a regulated instrument under the EU's Markets in Financial Instruments Directive 2004/39/EC (MiFID),[81] thus there are no licensing requirements for companies that deal in bitcoins to obtain a license from the Malta Financial Services Authority.[82]

---

[78] Giulia Aranguena De La Paz, *Bitcoin, moneta virtuale e mezzo di pagamento reale: l'UE meglio degli USA? (In teoria, sì)* [*Bitcoin, Virtual Currency and Actual Payment Method: Is the EU Better than the USA (In Theory, Yes)*], KEY4BIZ (July 8, 2013), http://www.key4biz.it/News/2013/07/08/Net_economy/Bitcoin_moneta_virtuale_e_mezzo_di_pagamento_reale_218903.html.

[79] Summary of Bank of Japan Press Conference, at 10 (Dec. 24, 2013), http://www.boj.or.jp/announcements/press/kaiken_2013/kk1312c.pdf (in Japanese).

[80] Mark Smalley, *Bank Negara's Officially Unofficial Statement on Bitcoin Is No Statement*, BETANOMICS (Nov. 4, 2013), http://betanomics.asia/blog/bank-negara-malaysian-government-unoffical-bitcoin-statement.

[81] Directive 2004/39/EC of the European Parliament and of the Council of 21 April 2004 on Markets in Financial Instruments Amending Council Directives 85/611/EEC and 93/6/EEC and Directive 2000/12/EC of the European Parliament and of the Council and Repealing Council Directive 93/22/EEC, 2004 O.J. (L 145) 1, http://eur-lex.europa.eu/LexUriServ/LexUriServ.do?uri=CELEX:32004L0039:EN:HTML.

[82] Charles Casar, *Malta Bitcoin Company*, CHETCUTI CAUCHI, http://www.ccmalta.com/publications/malta_bitcoin_company (last visited Jan. 8, 2014).

In October 2012, a Maltese company launched the first bitcoin hedge fund. The fund was "incorporated as a Bermuda exempted company and is registered as a segregated account company receiving funds at Citibank London."[83]

Netherlands

Virtual currencies such as bitcoins currently do not fall within the scope of the Act on Financial Supervision (Wet op het financieel toezicht) of the Netherlands, as the Dutch Minister of Finance, Jeroen Dijsselbloem, recently emphasized.[84] "The 'alternative virtual currency' [bitcoin] cannot be seen as 'electronic money,' " he stated, "because it fails the definition set by the Dutch law."[85] The Act defines "electronic money" as "a monetary value stored on an electronic device or stored on-distance in a central accounting record," and an "electronic money institution" as "a party, not being a bank, whose business it is to obtain the disposal of funds in exchange for which electronic money with which payments can be made is issued, also to parties other than the party issuing the electronic money."[86] Thus, under the Act, electronic money can be described as having the following features: it "is stored electronically; represents a claim on the person or organization who issues it; is issued in exchange for money, in order to make payments; and it can be used to pay both the issuer and others."[87] Because bitcoins "do not represent a claim on the issuer and they aren't necessarily issued in exchange for money, they aren't electronic money," a Dutch Internet lawyer, Arnoud Engelfriet, has explained.[88] Nor does Engelfriet consider bitcoins financial products, so value-added tax would be due on bitcoins received.[89]

---

[83] Jon Matonis, *First Bitcoin Hedge Fund Launches from Malta*, FORBES (Aug. 3, 2013), http://www.forbes.com/sites/jonmatonis/2013/03/08/first-bitcoin-hedge-fund-launches-from-malta/.

[84] The Minister recently pointed this out in response to written questions posed by the Dutch parliament. *See Minister Dijsselbloem: virtuele valuta's zoals Bitcoin vallen niet onder toezicht AFM [Authority for Financial Markets] en DNB [Dutch Central Bank] [Minister Dijsselbloem: Virtual Currencies Like Bitcoin Do Not Fall Under the Supervision [of the] AFM and DNB]*, AFM (Dec. 20, 2013), http://www.afm.nl/nl/nieuws/2013/dec/toezicht-bitcoins.aspx. Ministry of Finance, Beantwoording Kamervragen over het gebruik van en toezicht op nieuwe digitale betaalmiddelen zoals de Bitcoin [Answers to Parliamentary Questions on the Use and Control of New Digital Means of Payment Such as Bitcoin] (Dec. 19, 2013), available on the Government of the Netherlands website, at http://www.rijksoverheid.nl/onderwerpen/betalingen-en-beleggingsverzekeringen/documenten-en-publicaties/kamerstukken/2013/12/19/beantwoording-kamervragen-over-het-gebruik-van-en-toezicht-op-nieuwe-digitale-betaalmiddelen-zoals-de-bitcoin.html.

[85] Branko Collin, *Bitcoin Income Shall Be Taxed, Dijsselbloem Says,* 24 ORANGES (June 17, 2013), http://www.24oranges.nl/2013/06/17/bitcoin-income-shall-be-taxed-dijsselbloem-says/.

[86] Wet op het financieel toezicht [Act on Financial Supervision] (Sept. 28, 2006, as last amended Sept. 19, 2013, in force on Jan. 1, 2014) § 1:1, http://wetten.overheid.nl/BWBR0020368/geldigheidsdatum_31-12-2013 (Neth.); unofficial English translation as of Apr. 1, 2009, http://www.rijksoverheid.nl/documenten-en-publicaties/brieven/2009/11/16/engelse-vertaling-van-de-wft.html (click on "Download 'Engelse vertaling van de Wft' " PDF document).

[87] Collin, *supra* note 85.

[88] *Id.*

[89] *Id.* A "financial product" is defined under the Act on Financial Supervision as "an investment object; a current account including the ancillary payment facilities; electronic money; a financial instrument; credit; a savings account including the ancillary savings facilities; an insurance not being a reinsurance; or another product to be specified by Decree." Act on Financial Supervision § 1:1.

In response to a question from the Dutch Parliament as to the likelihood of the formal legal definition of electronic money being revised in anticipation that virtual currencies will increasingly function as money, the Minister of Finance indicated that such a change is not yet desirable, given the bitcoin's limited scope, relatively low level of acceptance, and limited relationship to the real economy. He emphasized that currently, despite the watchful eye of government authorities on the future development of virtual currencies, in principle the consumer is solely responsible for their use.[90]

The Dutch Central Bank (De Nederlandsche Bank, DNB) recently called attention to the risks posed by the purchase of virtual currencies, including bitcoins and litecoins,[91] and warned consumers to be wary.[92] It noted that the development of such currencies is growing but that exchange rates are volatile and that the DNB does not supervise them.[93] The former President of the DNB, Nout Wellink, has called dealings in bitcoins a bubble that is "pure speculation" and "hype" and "worse than the tulip mania" of the seventeenth century because "at least then you got a tulip [at the end], now you get nothing."[94]

New Zealand

The website of the Reserve Bank of New Zealand states the following:

> The Reserve Bank of New Zealand Act prohibits the issuance of bank notes and coins by any party other than the Reserve Bank. However, the Reserve Bank has no direct power over any form of alternative payments medium.
>
> Non-banks do not need our approval for schemes that involve the storage and/or transfer of value (such as 'bitcoin') – so long as they do not involve the issuance of physical circulating currency (notes and coins).[95]

---

[90] Ministry of Finance, *supra* note 84, Question/Reply 5.

[91] Litecoin is a peer-to-peer Internet currency based on the Bitcoin protocol but differing from Bitcoin in that it provides faster transaction confirmations and can be more efficiently mined with consumer-grade hardware. *What is Litecoin?*, LITECOIN, https://litecoin.org/ (last visited Jan. 24, 2014).

[92] *Consumers Should Be Aware of the Risks of Virtual Currencies,* DE NEDERLANDSCHE BANK (Dec. 3, 2013), http://www.dnb.nl/en/news/news-and-archive/nieuws-2013/dnb300672.jsp#.

[93] *Id.*

[94] Alex Hern, *Bitcoin Hype Worse Than 'Tulip Mania', Says Dutch Central Banker,* THE GUARDIAN (Dec. 4, 2013), http://www.theguardian.com/technology/2013/dec/04/bitcoin-bubble-tulip-dutch-banker. As of December 5, 2013, a partly tongue-in-cheek article in *The Atlantic* noted that "you can buy more than 700 tulips with one bitcoin. That's a precipitous rise in value—at the beginning of October 2013, you couldn't even buy 90 tulips with one bitcoin. And two years ago? A single bitcoin could buy you almost exactly two measly tulips." Robinson Meyer, *How Many Tulips Can You Buy With One Bitcoin?*, THE ATLANTIC (Dec. 5, 2013), http://www.theatlantic.com/technology/archive/2013/12/how-many-tulips-can-you-buy-with-one-bitcoin/282062/.

[95] *Notes and Coins Frequently Asked Questions*, RESERVE BANK OF NEW ZEALAND, http://www.rbnz.govt.nz/notes_and_coins/0094941.html (last visited Dec. 23, 2013).

On December 11, 2013, *The Wall Street Journal* reported that the assistant governor of the Reserve Bank had urged the country's banks and businesses to exercise caution with regard to the bitcoin, saying "[y]ou have to worry about where's the supply, how it's controlled, how it's monitored. Who knows at this point? There is still a lot for the world to learn on this issue."[96] New Zealand's Commerce Commission says the bitcoin is covered by the Fair Trading Act and the Commerce Act.[97]

Nicaragua

It appears that Nicaragua has not yet promulgated any legislation regulating bitcoins, nor has the Central Bank of Nicaragua issued any rulings or guidelines on the subject. However, news reports indicate that bitcoins are being used in the country.

The Nicaraguan daily *El Nuevo Diario* reported on January 13, 2014, that an American banker, Greg Simon, recently bought a 1,200-square-meter plot of land in San Juán del Sur, one of the most important tourist areas in Nicaragua, for 80 bitcoins, currently the equivalent of about US$72,000. Simon is reportedly interested in promoting the use of bitcoins in Nicaragua and advanced some ideas related to their use. The article indicated that the real estate agency involved in the transaction, Century 21 Nica Life Realty, has received many emails from people welcoming the sale and from others interested in using bitcoins to buy land in San Juán del Sur.[98]

Poland

The use of the bitcoin in Poland is not regulated by a legal act at present. On December 18, 2013, the Warsaw School of Economics conducted a conference entitled "Poland – A Bitcoin Superpower: Opportunities and Threats." According to information published on the school's Facebook page, an official representative of the Polish Ministry of Finance, Szymon Wozniak, participated in the conference and stated that the Ministry of Finance does not view the bitcoin as an illegal means of payment, but also cannot recognize it as a legal currency.[99]

On December 21, 2013, the Russian website Coinspot.ru reported that at the Warsaw conference, Wozniak said that Polish financial institutions define their position on digital currencies in accordance with the position of the European regulatory financial institutions. He was cited as saying that Poland "does not attempt to prevent the development of Bitcoin. . . . [W]e expect that

---

[96] Rebecca Howard, *New Zealand Central Bank Joins Others in Warning on Bitcoins*, THE WALL STREET JOURNAL (Dec. 11, 2013), http://blogs.wsj.com/economics/2013/12/11/new-zealand-central-bank-joins-others-in-warning-on-bitcoins/?mod=WSJBlog.

[97] Laura Walters, *Bitcoin: Beauty or Bubble?*, STUFF.CO.NZ (Dec. 28, 2013), http://www.stuff.co.nz/technology/digital-living/30008862/bitcoin-beauty-or-bubble.

[98] Andrea Sepúlveda, *Nicaragua Ya Acepta Moneda Virtual Bitcoin*, EL NUEVO DIARIO (Jan. 13, 2014), http://www.elnuevodiario.com.ni/nacionales/307477.

[99] Wojciech Milczarek et. al., *Polska potęgą bitcoin – szanse i zagrożenia* [*Poland – A Bitcoin Superpower: Opportunities and Threats*], SEMINARIUM BITCOIN CLUB SGH, https://www.facebook.com/events/1380771012175255 (last visited Jan. 16, 2014).

the users will decide by themselves if the government needs to regulate and protect this area or everything shall stay as it is."[100]

Wozniak was more certain about the taxation of bitcoin transactions. He said that all types of income must be taxed under Polish law, and the law makes no distinction among the types of payments used to conduct transactions, including bitcoin payments. According to him, all income received from bitcoin transactions is subject to reporting and taxation.[101]

Portugal

On November 22, 2013, the Bank of Portugal issued a press release addressing bitcoins[102] in which the Bank makes reference to a recent study of the European Central Bank (ECB). The study asserts that Bitcoin is considered a bidirectional virtual currency payment model (virtual currency scheme type 3) in which users can both buy and sell virtual currency with legal tender and with which they can purchase goods and services in both the real and virtual worlds.[103]

The press release states that because there is no central authority to ensure the finality and irrevocability of payment orders and no certainty of their acceptance as a means of payment, bitcoins cannot be considered a safe currency. Their issuance is made by unregulated and unsupervised entities and is therefore not subject to any prudential requirements. The system is also not subject to any oversight activity. Users bear all the risk, since there is no fund to protect depositors/investors.[104]

The bitcoin has no specific legal framework in Portugal, either at the level of its creation or at the level of its use, that defines clear rights and responsibilities for all parties involved in the payment model. As its creation is decentralized and there is no "owner" of the system, it is difficult to define the jurisdiction under which procedures and rules applicable to the model should be established.[105]

In its report, the ECB recognizes the existence of Bitcoin as an innovative model of virtual currency. However, neither the ECB nor the Bank of Portugal oversees the issuance or use of bitcoins in Portugal or in Europe.[106]

---

[100] *Poland Does Not Consider Bitcoin Transactions Illegal*, COINSPOT.RU (Dec. 21, 2013), http://coinspot.ru/news/polsha-ne-schitaet-bitkoin-tranzakcii-nezakonnymi/ (in Russian).

[101] *Id.*

[102] Press Release, Banco de Portugal, Meios de Pagamento: Bitcoin [Bank of Portugal, Means of Payment: Bitcoin] (Nov. 22, 2013), http://www.bportugal.pt/pt-PT/OBancoeoEurosistema/Esclarecimentospublicos/Paginas/meiosdepagamento.aspx.

[103] European Central Bank, *supra* note 40.

[104] Press Release, Banco de Portugal, *supra* note 102.

[105] *Id.*

[106] *Id.*

The press release reports that Bitcoin is understood as a payment model of bidirectional virtual currency, in which the virtual currency competes with legal tender (e.g., the euro or the dollar). At present, although its issuance and acceptance has been growing, it seems that the bitcoin's relationship with the real economy is still limited, with bitcoins exhibiting both low trading volumes and low levels of acceptance. As this reality could change substantially in the future, the European central banks are monitoring the phenomenon and may eventually recognize and act on payment models of virtual currency.[107]

Russia

There are at present no legal acts that specifically regulate the use of bitcoins in the Russian Federation. According to a report prepared by the Russian law firm Tolkachev and Partners, however, the use of bitcoins can be restricted according to article 140 of the Russian Civil Code, which recognizes the Russian ruble as the exclusive means of payment in the Russian Federation and requires that all prices for financial transactions conducted in Russia be defined in rubles.[108] According to the report, if the bitcoin is considered by the parties to be a foreign currency or external security for the purposes of a particular transaction, such a transaction can be recognized as an illegal currency operation subject to prosecution under the Russian law on administrative responsibility.[109]

German Gref, president of largest Russian government-owned bank, Sberbank, stated in a recent interview that Russian authorities are monitoring developments related to the bitcoin.[110] He said that global regulation of virtual currencies will be needed in the near future, and he did not exclude the possibility of Russian involvement in this process. Additionally, he said that the issuance of virtual currency can be initiated in Russia based on one of the existing national online payment systems.[111]

Singapore

In September 2013 a spokesman of Singapore's central bank, the Monetary Authority of Singapore (MAS), reportedly warned consumers to "be wary of . . . trading [in bitcoins]."[112] According to the news report, the MAS spokesman told the media that "[i]f Bitcoin ceases to operate, there may not be an identifiable party responsible for refunding [consumers'] monies or for them to seek recourse."[113]

---

[107] *Id.*

[108] Artem Tolkachev & Kseniia Osipova, *Possibilities and Risks of Using Bitcoin in Russia*, ATPLAW.RU (Aug. 29, 2013), http://www.atplaw.ru/useful/articles/vozmozhnosti-i-riski-ispolzovaniya-bitkoin-v-rossii.html (in Russian).

[109] *Id.*

[110] *Gref: Development of Virtual Currencies Cannot Be Stopped*, NEWSLAND.RU (Dec. 14, 2013), http://newsland. com/news/detail/id/1293000/ (in Russian).

[111] *Id.*

[112] Irene Tham, *Bitcoin Users Beware: MAS*, STRAITS TIMES (Sept. 22, 2013), *available at* ASIAONE BUSINESS, http://business.asiaone.com/news/bitcoin-users-beware-mas.

[113] *Id.*

In December 2013, the MAS reportedly decided not to intervene on the question of whether businesses can accept bitcoins as a means of transacting goods and services.[114] In an email to a Singapore-based bitcoin trading platform, according to the news report, the MAS stated that "[w]hether or not businesses accept Bitcoins in exchange for their goods and services is a commercial decision in which MAS does not intervene."[115]

In January 2014, the Inland Revenue Authority of Singapore reportedly laid out tax advice regarding the purchase, sale, and exchange of bitcoins for local businesses and individuals in an email response to queries on bitcoins:[116] "Bitcoin itself is not considered a good, nor does it qualify as money or currency, according to the IRAS and under Singapore's GST [Goods and Services Tax] Act. Instead, the supply of Bitcoins is examined under GST and varies according to how the service is provided."[117]

Slovenia

On December 23, 2013, the Ministry of Finance of the Republic of Slovenia issued a formal opinion about the status of the bitcoin and other virtual currencies in response to a request from the Tax Administration of the Republic of Slovenia.[118] The opinion states that the bitcoin is not a monetary means under Slovenian law and not a financial instrument. According to the Ministry of Finance, the existing legislative framework does not contain provisions applicable to businesses involved in bitcoin trading.[119] However, the Ministry stressed that taxation of bitcoin income still warrants review on an individual basis.

Commenting on the opinion, the Slovenian news service Beforeitsnews.com stated that it is necessary to determine who actually generates the income and to classify what sort of income is being generated:

> Thus some income will be taxed. Income made by individuals is subject to standard income tax provisions, irrespective of the form. Bitcoin income will apparently be taxed by measuring the bitcoin/euro exchange at the time of the transaction. Personal income tax is not paid on capital gains. Individuals who generate income by selling bitcoins will

---

[114] Terence Lee, *Singapore Government Decides Not to Interfere with Bitcoin*, TECHINASIA (Dec. 23, 2013), http://www.techinasia.com/singapore-government-decides-interfere-bitcoin/.

[115] *Id.*

[116] Michael Lee, *Singapore Issues Tax Guidance on Bitcoins*, ZDNET (Jan. 9, 2014), http://www.zdnet.com/singapore-issues-tax-guidance-on-bitcoins-7000024966/.

[117] *Id.*

[118] Tax Treatment of Virtual Currency Operations DOH-2 and CITA-2, REPUBLIC OF SLOVENIA, MINISTRY OF FINANCE: TAX ADMINISTRATION (Dec. 23, 2013), http://www.durs.gov.si/si/davki_predpisi_in_pojasnila/dohodnina_pojasnila/dohodek_iz_kapitala/dobicek_iz_kapitala/vrednostni_papirji_in_delezi_v_gospodarskih_druzbah_zadrugah_in_drugih_oblikah_organiziranja_ter_investicijski_kuponi/davcna_obravnava_poslovanja_z_virtualno_valuto_po_zdoh_2_in_zddpo_2/ (in Slovenian).

[119] *Id.*

not pay income tax. At that [sic] profits derived from trading and mining Bitcoin are taxed as income under the provisions of Slovenian personal income legislation.[120]

Spain

Bitcoins have not yet been regulated in Spain and are not considered to be legal currency since they are not issued by the government's monetary authority. However, they may be considered digital goods or things under the Civil Code,[121] and transactions with bitcoins may be governed by the rules of barter contained in the Civil Code,[122]according to the analysis of one Spanish law firm.[123] Merchants who accept bitcoins are required to issue an invoice with value-added tax in euros.[124]

Spain was the second country in the world to seize bitcoins during an investigation of fraudulent transactions conducted with bitcoins, according to a November 2013 report by *El Mundo*.[125]

South Korea

There are at present no laws in South Korea regulating the use of the Bitcoin system. However, the president of the Bank of Korea recommended at a press conference on December 12, 2013, that the bitcoin be regulated in the future.[126]

Taiwan

As of January 13, 2013, Taiwan had not passed any legislation regulating the use of bitcoins. On December 30, 2013, the Central Bank of the Republic of Taiwan and the Financial Supervisory Commission (FSC) issued a warning to the public about the risks in dealing with bitcoins. The regulators said the bitcoin is not a real currency, but a "highly speculative virtual commodity." The general public was warned about the specific risks associated with accepting, trading, or holding bitcoins. If financial institutions use bitcoins, according to the warning, the Central

---

[120] *Slovenia Clarified the Question of Bitcoin Taxation*, BEFOREITSNEWS.COM (Dec. 25, 2013), http://beforeitsnews. com/economy/2013/12/slovenia-clarified-the-question-of-bitcoin-taxation-2581938.html.

[121] CÓDIGO CIVIL [CIVIL CODE] arts. 335, 337 & 345 (July 25, 1889, as amended), BOLETÍN OFICIAL DEL ESTADO, http://boe.es/buscar/act.php?id=BOE-A-1889-4763 (Spain).

[122] *Id.* art. 1538.

[123] Pablo Fernández Burgueño, *12 Cosas que Deberías Saber Antes de Usar Bitcoins (La Ley y el Bitcoin)* [*Twelve Things You Should Know Before Using Bitcoins (The Law and Bitcoin)*], ABANLEX ABOGADOS (Nov. 27, 2013), http://www.abanlex.com/index.php?s=bitcoin (scroll down to find article).

[124] *Id.*

[125] Pablo Romero, *Así se Incauta la Policía de Bitcoins* [*This is How Bitcoins Are Seized by the Police*], EL MUNDO (Nov. 1, 2013), http://www.elmundo.es/tecnologia/2013/11/01/5270d45363fd3da7618b4576.html.

[126] *Hanun "chongbu pit'uk'oin kyuje mandu rora"* [*Bank of Korea: "Government Needs to Make Bitcoin Regulation"*], HANKOOKI (Dec. 27, 2013), http://economy.hankooki.com/lpage/economy/201312/e201312271 5412370070.htm.

Bank and the FSC may, in accordance with laws and regulations, take necessary regulatory actions at the appropriate time.[127]

Thailand

According to news reports, the Bank of Thailand ruled the bitcoin illegal on July 29, 2013.[128] However, it appears that "it issued a preliminary ruling that using bitcoins . . . was illegal because of a lack of existing laws" in the case of a currency-exchange license application by Bitcoin Co. Ltd. Other businesses that have licenses have continued operating bitcoin exchanges in Thailand.[129]

Turkey

No formal regulations on the bitcoin exist in Turkey. The bitcoin, according to a press release issued in November 2013 by the country's Banking Regulation and Supervision Agency, is not considered electronic money within the scope of the newly enacted Law on Payment and Securities Reconciliation Systems, Payment Services, and Electronic Money Institutions,[130] "and thus its surveillance and supervision are not possible within the frame of the Law."[131] The press release goes on to warn the public that the lack of identification of the parties involved in bitcoin or similar virtual money transactions "creates a suitable environment for these virtual monies to be used in illegal activities."[132] It adds that the bitcoin or similar virtual money also poses risks because its market value may be extremely volatile; it may be stolen from a digital wallet, lost, or illegally used without the owners' knowledge; and it may be subject to operational errors resulting from irreversible transactions or to abuses inflicted by malicious vendors.[133]

One Turkish commentator points out that because Bitcoin is independent of any control mechanism, it is not possible to freeze or seize Bitcoin accounts.[134] Some financial experts in Turkey liken Bitcoin, in terms of its features and pattern of development, to Tulip mania in

---

[127] 比特幣並非貨幣，接受者務請注意風險承擔問題 [*Bitcoin Is Not Real Currency; Accepters Please Look to the Risks*] (Dec. 30, 2013), http://www.cbc.gov.tw/ct.asp?xItem=43531&ctNode=302.

[128] Jake Maxwell Watts, *Thailand's Bitcoin Ban Is Not Quite What It Seems*, QUARTZ (July 31, 2013), http://qz.com/110164/thailands-infamous-bitcoin-crackdown-is-not-quite-what-it-seems/.

[129] *Id. See also*, Bangkok Pundit, *Has Bitcoin Really Been Banned in Thailand?*, ASIAN CORRESPONDENT (July 31, 2013), http://asiancorrespondent.com/111332/has-bitcoin-been-banned-from-thailand/.

[130] Ödeme ve Menkul Kıymet Mutabakat Sistemleri, Ödeme Hizmetleri ve Elektronik Para Kuruluşları Hakkında Kanun [Law on Payment and Securities Reconciliation Systems, Payment Services, and Electronic Money Institutions] (June 20, 2013), No. 6493, 28690 RESMÎ GAZETE [OFFICIAL GAZETTE] (June 27, 2013), http://www.resmigazete.gov.tr/eskiler/2013/06/20130627-14.htm (Turkey).

[131] Press Release, 2013/32, Banking Regulation and Supervision Agency, [untitled] (Nov. 25, 2013), http://www.bddk.org.tr/websitesi/english/Announcements/Press_Releases/12585bitcoin_press_release_eng_3.pdf.

[132] *Id.*

[133] *Id.*

[134] Ceren Savaser, *Bitcoin and Taxation Under Turkish Legislation*, HG.ORG LEGAL RESOURCES (Dec. 9, 2013), http://www.hg.org/ article.asp?id=31755.

Holland, the Mississippi balloon in France, or the Enron or mortgage balloons in the United States, because the bitcoin "has no use value, but only exchange value."[135] Moreover, in their view, because it has no intrinsic worth other than what others are willing to pay for it, "it is always in a bubble."[136]

Nevertheless, bitcoin use is apparently flourishing in Turkey. There is a Turkish Lira-Bitcoin exchange, called BTCTurk, and leftover foreign currency can be exchanged at the Istanbul Ataturk Airport for bitcoins through a Traveler's BOX, a machine like an ATM.[137] BTCTurk, which was launched in July 2013, is reportedly the first company in Turkey "to enable the exchange of Turkish lira for bitcoin and vice versa."[138]

United Kingdom

There has been no official statement published on the Bank of England's website regarding its position towards Bitcoin. In the latest quarterly reports from the Bank, Bitcoin is expressly excluded.[139] The government of the United Kingdom has stated that the bitcoin is currently unregulated.[140] A high-level review of bitcoin use took place in the summer of 2013, at which time concerns were raised as to the lack of transparency with the use of the coin, but it was left unregulated.[141]

While bitcoins are not regulated, it has been reported that Her Majesty's Revenue and Customs has classed bitcoins as "single purpose vouchers," rendering any sales of them liable to a value-added tax of 10–20%. This has been strongly criticized by those selling bitcoins as being "a show stopper for the UK Bitcoin industry."[142] There is no specific reference on Her Majesty's Revenue and Customs site to bitcoins.

Several Freedom of Information requests for information about meetings involving discussions of the bitcoin at different government departments and bodies have been rejected in accordance

---

[135] *Id.*

[136] *Id.*

[137] Maria Santos, *Travelers BOX at Turkish Airport Allows You to Exchange Currency Leftovers for Bitcoin* BITCOIN EXAMINER.ORG(Nov. 18, 2013), http://bitcoinexaminer.org/travelers-box-at-turkish-airport-allows-you-to-exchange-currency-leftovers-for-bitcoin/. The article includes a picture of the Travelers BOX.

[138] Emily Spaven, *BTCTurk Becomes the First Turkish Lira-to-Bitcoin Exchange*, COINDESK (July 31, 2013), http://www.coindesk.com/btcturk-becomes-the-first-turkish-lira-to-bitcoin-exchange/.

[139] Mona Naqvi & James Southgate, Bank of England, *Banknotes, Local Currencies and Central Bank Objectives*, 53: 4 QUARTERLY BULLETIN 319 n. 3 (2013), http://www.bankofengland.co.uk/publications/Documents/quarterlybulletin/2013/qb1304.pdf.

[140] *Banking: Bitcoins*, PARL. DEB., H.L. (5th ser.) 4013 (Dec. 18, 2013), http://www.publications.parliament.uk/pa/ld201314/ldhansrd/text/131218w0001.htm (U.K.).

[141] Jane Wild, *UK Taxmen, Police and Spies Look at Bitcoin Threat*, FINANCIAL TIMES (London) (May 13, 2013), http://www.ft.com/cms/s/2/42ca6762-bbfc-11e2-82df-00144feab7de.html#axzz2pdQoiDZO.

[142] Tom Gullen, *The Challenge of Being a Bitcoin Trader*, FINANCIAL SERVICES CLUB BLOG (Nov. 13, 2013), http://thefinanser.co.uk/fsclub/2013/11/the-challenge-of-being-a-bitcoin-trader.html.

with sections 31 and 35 of the Freedom of Information Act.[143] Section 31 provides that information is exempt from the provisions of the Freedom of Information Act if it will prejudice law enforcement, with the reasons cited as "prejudic[ing] the activities of one or more of the law enforcement agencies." Section 35 of the Act provides that information is exempt if it relates to the formulation or development of government policy.[144]

---

[143] Freedom of Information Act. 2000, c. 36, http://www.legislation.gov.uk/ukpga/2000/ 36/contents (U.K.).

[144] Gullen, *supra* note 142.

www.ingramcontent.com/pod-product-compliance
Lightning Source LLC
Chambersburg PA
CBHW081824170526
45167CB00008B/3533